Reflections Of A
Mississippi Magnolia

**This book is dedicated to
my parents**

**Dr. James H. Neely
and
Mrs. Elaine Kilgore Neely**

*Thank you for giving me
the two most important things
you can give a child —*

ROOTS and WINGS.

Reflections
Of A
Mississippi Magnolia

A Life in Poems

— ◆ —

by
Patricia Neely-Dorsey

— ◆ —

GrantHouse Publishers
2007

ISBN: 978-0-9796294-2-6

Copies of this book are available from:

Patricia Neely-Dorsey
1196 CR 681
Saltillo, MS 38866
(901) 848-6800
Email: magnoliagirl21@yahoo.com

Published by
GrantHouse Publishers
2101 Green Leaf Drive, Jonesboro, AR 72401
TEL: 870-934-0418
E-mail: granthousepub@aol.com
WEB: granthousepublishers.com

Cover design by Rainey Scott
Author's photo by Merlin Conoway, Jr.

Printed in the United States of America

Table of Contents

Southern Life

Country Living

Childhood Memories

Family History

Getting Personal

Intimacies

Summing Things Up

Foreword

When I think of how this book came to be and how it finally arrived to you the reader, I think of the words of the song "The Long and Winding Road". Though most of the poems in this book were written within a span of six months (February 2007-August 2007), they've all been in the making from very early in my life. My mother gave me a passionate love for reading and writing, and my father gave me an appreciation for poetry and great literature, especially that of African American origin. Then in my late teens, in the early 80's, John Campbell came on the scene in my life in the form of a coach and teacher with John Campbell Productions, a modeling troupe and sort of finishing school.

John influenced and affected how I saw myself as far as the talent that I had inside, my potential and the heights to which I could soar. John saw greatness inside of me and always encouraged me to dream big... really big, and to go after those dreams. He even had his own dreams for me and would often convey them in long heartfelt rap sessions on his couch. He would tell me about his life growing up in the Delta, about ideas for inventions he had, and about traveling on the road and being the personal valet for his big brother Little Milton, a famous blues singer.

Though John could be very strict and pushy, and sometimes hurtful to my tender young ego, he made me look beyond my immediate reach and dare to think outside of the box. Actually, he helped me to see that for me there should be no box. The sky is the limit.

When John left Tupelo, many years elapsed and we lost contact. Fate saw fit that our paths should cross again. At a book signing of his first book at Reed's Gumtree Bookstore, in Historic Downtown Tupelo, all the years came flooding back. It certainly was not a chance reunion in that I had just recently moved back to Tupelo from Memphis, TN, after residing there for almost twenty years. If I had still been in Memphis, I certainly would not have seen the notice of his book signing and would not have been in Tupelo in the middle of the week to attend.

After talking to John about my writings and showing them to him the next day, it took only two months from that fateful meeting for this, my first book of poetry, to be published. It would be exactly one year from the time I wrote my first poem. John gets things done! He also fancies himself somewhat of a comedian. He often jokes, "I almost quit school in the third grade because they had recess and I don't play." You never lied, brother! Thank you, John Campbell, for making me believe that dreams really do come true and for helping a little Mississippi Magnolia girl realize one of hers.

Patricia Neely-Dorsey

About My Writings

I always hesitate to call myself a poet. I feel more like a vessel or a conduit through which the poems flow. I never intentionally sat down to write any of them. They all came to me, fully complete and neatly packaged, title and all. I just put them down on paper. Because of this, I tell people that none of the poems took more than five to ten minutes to write, maybe fifteen, at the most, for the longer ones.

There are only two poems in the whole book for which I put words together from a chosen topic. After I had written maybe ten to twenty poems, I was telling a friend that I really didn't think I could just come up with the words to form a good poem because of the way they just came to me. So, my friend gave me two topics: a tree and an animal, and I began to write. Those poems came to be "The Cat" and "The Magnolia Tree." As I stated earlier in the foreword, most of the poems were written in a span of six months (February 2007 - August 2007). Ninety percent of the poems were written in February and March of 2007.

I woke up on Valentine's Day 2007 and had "Our Place" in my head, complete from beginning to end. The words were forcefully dancing around in my head, so I quickly found a pen and paper to write them down. To this day, it remains one of my favorites, along with "Let's" and "Mississippi Man."

Also, most of my poems were conceived and written in my car. Sometimes the words would come crowding into my head and I would have to try to scribble them down as best as I could. I have little scraps of paper everywhere with poems on them. "Mississippi Through and Through" came to me as I was enjoying the beautiful scenery with my car packed to the brim, and my son asleep on the backseat, as I was moving back to Tupelo on a bright sunny day in August 2007.

As you can see, I am so proud of where I come from, so happy with the life I've lived, and totally enamored with the southern way of life. I hope that you find as much joy in reading my poems as I have found in bringing them to you.

Patricia Neely-Dorsey

Acknowledgments/Special Thanks

To my most loving, devoted husband, James, who has been there for me through thick and thin. Thank you for always accepting me just as I am,and always encouraging me to 'do the right thing'.

To my son, Henry, who is my heart. You have taught me the true meaning of love. I love seeing your personality develop and watching you grow into a fine young man.

To my parents, Dr. and Mrs. James Neely. Thank you for being the best parents on the planet. You provided me with a fairytale childhood. Thank you for always supporting me in all my endeavors.

To my brother, Attorney Brian Neely, who has always been my champion and protector. Thank you for always looking out for your little sister.

Thank you to my sorority sisters of Alpha Kappa Alpha Inc., Nu Sigma Omega Chapter, for all of your continuing encouragement and support.

To Alvita Johnson, who has always been that voice of reason in my life, even when I was being a 'wild child' trying to find my way.

To Blanche Ray, a friend forever, even though you didn't sing at my wedding. (smile)

To Damita "Chelle" Tucker, I have always admired you from a child, and even more so now. You are my role model for what the ideal Christian woman, wife and mother should look like, act like and be. I want to be just like you 'when I grow up.' (smile)

To the Agnews, my second family, who allowed me to experience 'true' country living.

To the Neely and Kilgore Clans, you are part of all that I am and ever hope to be.

To my cousin, Drustella Neely, who has always been the big sister that I never had. Thank you for all of your resources in helping to get my book together.

To my aunt, Robbie Neely Jones, the true fashion and decorating diva of the family. You taught me everything I know in those areas. Thank you for always giving of yourself so generously.

To all of my brothers and sisters in Christ, especially the North Green Street and Boulevard congregations. Thank you for nurturing me along the way.

To Brenda Garrison, who always gave me wise counsel, even when I didn't want to hear it. Thank you for taking me under your wing. You are a true modern day Proverbs 31 woman.

To Joyce Savage, a fellow poet and author, you inspired me to have my own poems published.

To Saundra Slocum, one of the most resourceful people I know. You truly taught me and showed me, "Where there's a will, there's a way."

To Gwen Jackson, the yard sale/ thrift shop queen. Thank you for always coming to the rescue… anyone's rescue. You are a tireless servant with a heart of gold. You've always been there for me... except when you chickened out on 'that tatoo thing.' (smile)

To Malcolm Jackson, Jr., who kept telling me, "These poems are really good." I hope everyone else thinks so too. Thank you for encouraging me to put them out there.

To Malcolm Jackson, III at Smoothie King, in Memphis TN, Thank you for the best Smoothies around. I still say that we desperately need a Smoothie King in Tupelo. They don't know what they are missing.

To Jurice Cole, a dear friend and confidant, I really miss my weekly 'therapy' sessions with you. So many people depend on your wisdom and strength and I am one of them.

To Mrs. Earline Dobbs, thank you for being so good at what you do. You have "saved" so many of us so many times. Thank you for being so gracious, calm, patient and kind. Thank you for all of your help over the years.

To Russell Freeman, Thank you so much for all of your advice and mentoring. You taught me some valuable lessons. I wouldn't mind if some of those famous hot wings would make their way down to Tupelo (hint, hint).

To Terrance Potlow, a man of big dreams. Thank you for inspiring me to dream big and aim high.

To Mrs. Gloria Sims, my second Mom in the 'city', I can't count the number of times you took me in when Mom and Dad were out of town. Thank you for making me a part of your big family.

To Phyllis Sims Cobb, you always told me to wrap up, put on a sweater and wear some stockings. I didn't listen, and I'm paying for it now. Thank you for all of your care and concern over the years.

To Fannie Cleveland, my other second mother in the 'city'. I practically grew up in your house. Thank you for always being there for me.

To the Summer Avenue crew of Southeast Mental Health Center. Thank you for listening to the poems in my book before any of us even knew there would be any book.

To Tamiko Woodall. You are the glue that kept everything together and running smoothly. You are invaluable.

To Tekela Cooper, the sweetest and most generous person anyone could ever know (undercover). Don't worry, I won't let your secret out. (smile)

To Suzanne Shelton, thank you for your level-headedness and positive attitude. I miss exchanging our Henry and Jesse stories and new found revelations of 'old age'.

To Chiquita "Qui Qui" Herrod, the baby of the bunch. Your bubbly personality is infectious. Thanks for being my faithful Curves workout partner and shopping buddy.

To Tanci Parker, The Diva, with a capital D. You are the epitome of Fabulosity. I can truly say I have NEVER met ANYONE like you. You are truly one of a kind and after you they broke the mold.

To Andromeda Ward, the eyebrow expert, thank you for lighting up everyone's world with that smile and laugh. And, thank you for making me "cute" with those tweezers.

To Annie Helen DePriest, one of the best beauticians around. You are the only one who ever "really" knew what to do with my hair. I will always consider you a friend.

To Elizabeth "Baby Sis" Reno. Thank you for taking me under your wing and "schooling" me, back in the day.

To Ms. Vera Dukes, a wonderful teacher, counselor and motivator. You encouraged every inkling of any literary talent that I had in my body. This book partly comes through you. Sorry that I couldn't be the great orator that you were trying to groom me to be. (smile)

To Mrs. Carolyn Long, my seventh grade English teacher. Thank you for always believing in me and encouraging my abilities. Do you still remember the Secret Pal gift, "Songs in the Key of Life"?

To Mr. James Tucker, my seventh grade science teacher, who always encouraged and challenged us to "dig deeper" for knowledge and truth.

To my high school crew (Hi Psi Phi), Rochelle, Verner, Misty, Jewel, Debra, and Shay, girls, we still got it going on. Love you all.

To Ms. Lillie Bell Johnson, a truly phenomenal woman and diligent, tireless, community worker and leader who has opened so many doors (and windows) for so many people. For me, you embody the true meaning of the word inspiration. You have taught me to never take NO for an answer. And , on top of all that you STILL LOOK GOOD.

To the impress staff at Office Max in Tupelo, MS., especially Kiersten Dilworth, thanks for all your help.

To Nathan Colvin at Staples in Tupelo, MS. You are wonderful! You really know your stuff!

To my publisher, Mr. George Grant, thank you so much for your patience and guidance in navigating me through the waters of getting a first book published. Every first time author should be so blessed to have someone like you to help them through the process. Thank-you for sharing your wisdom and knowledge (and sense of humor) so freely

Again, I would like to thank John W. Campbell for helping to make this dream project a reality. Thank you for holding my hand every step of the way.

Most of all, I want to thank God, the ultimate dream maker in my life. He has blessed me more than I could ever ask or imagine.

Psalms 37:4 -- "Delight thyself in the Lord and He will give you the desires of thine heart."

Southern Life

Southern Life

If you want a glimpse of Southern life,
Come close and walk with me;
I'll tell you all the simple things,
That you are sure to see.
You'll see mockingbirds and bumblebees,
Magnolia blossoms and dogwood trees,
Caterpillars on the step,
Wooden porches cleanly swept;
Watermelons on the vine,
Strong majestic Georgia pines;
Rocking chairs and front yard swings,
June bugs flying on a string;
Turnip greens and hot cornbread,
Coleslaw and barbecue;
Fried okra, fried corn, fried green tomatoes,
Fried pies and pickles, too.
There's ice cold tea that's syrupy sweet,
And cool green grass beneath your feet;
Catfish nipping in the lake,
And fresh young boys on the make.
You'll see all these things
And much, much more,
In a way of life that I adore.

Southern Man

There's nothing like a Southern man,
He's a man that you should know;
He's one to whom you'll find no equal,
Anywhere you go.
He has a sweet, molasses talk
And a slow, smooth, gliding walk.
He's got strong, firm hands that let you know,
Real work is nothing new;
He has no problem with the fact,
That he should provide for you.
There are certain kinds of values
This man is sure to hold
His love of home and family
Is sure to not grow cold.
He'll deeply love his mother
It's a bond that's always there
All throughout his life this man
Will show her tender care.
He's one that you can count on,
To do the manly things;
He'll change the tire and check the oil,
And fix the back yard swing.
But underneath a tough exterior,
A gentle soul lies too;
He's one who'll rock the baby,
And even cook a meal or two,
On Sundays he'll sit beside you singing,
On the same church pew.
There's nothing like a Southern man,
He's a rare and special kind;
If you look forever anywhere,
He's the best you'll ever find.

3

Sounds of Summer

Chirping of the crickets,
Buzzing of the bees,
Bullfrogs croaking in the pond,
Birds singing in the trees,
There are sounds of summer
That we all wait to hear;
It's part of what's so wonderful
About that time of year.

♦ ❖ ◆ ❖ ♦

Summer Night (Southern Style)

Moths flicker 'round the front porch light
Fireflies are taking flight
The sun has disappeared from sight
And all around the sounds of night.
Everything is warm and still
A sense of calm that one can feel
The moon shines bright over yonder hill
Can all this loveliness be real?

Mississippi Morning

I love a Mississippi morning,
On a summer's day;
Everything's so glorious
In the most delightful way.
The sun is peaking upward,
The earth begins to warm;
Magnificent works of nature,
Are simply just the norm.
There is a sense of wonderment
At how all things look so new;
The flowers glow with freshness,
From the past night's dew.
The beauty all around you,
Would take away your breath;
You'd feel you'd like to soak it in
Until there's nothing left.
There's nothing like a Mississippi morning,
On a summer's day;
It's such a grand production,
It seems we all should pay.

The Rules

Most Southern folk have rules we're taught,
From when we're very young;
And most of us throughout our lives,
To these rules have clung.
Life can be much easier,
When you know what to do or not;
And you're sure to learn a lot of them,
 If Southern parents you have got.
One of the first rules you come to know is
Children are to be seen and not heard;
It's best if you just sit down somewhere
Quietly as a bird.
You always say "Please" when you're asking,
And "Thank you", when you receive;
You address all your elders
As " Ma'am" or "Sir",
And if you don't do it, you'll grieve.
Don't touch anything in the store,
Keep your hands to yourself;
If it's not something you plan to buy,
Leave it soundly on the shelf.
Always say good morning,
Soon after you awake;
And always greet people pleasantly,
If friends you are to make.
Don't slam a door as you walk out,
"You don't live in a barn;"
You'd better close it gently,
Is what they'd always warn.

If you open a cabinet or anything,
Always close it back;
Once you do it repeatedly,
You'll always have the knack.
Don't call someone before 8 a.m.,
Or after ten at night;
If it's something you feel you must do,
It's an urge that you must fight.
Never ask for food when you visit,
Although the host may ask;
Sometimes it's best if you decline,
And let the moment pass.
These are just a very few of the things,
We Southerners are taught;
Without some rule for every occasion,
We are never caught.

Mississippi Man

I want to enjoy my Mississippi Man
On a Mississippi day
Soaking up some Mississippi sun.
I love the way we do
Mississippi things
And have our Mississippi fun.
He makes me laugh
A Mississippi laugh
And smile
A Mississippi smile.
I guess, if he would ask me to,
I'd run
A Mississippi Mile.

Local Color

In every small town there are people
Who act very strange,
For one reason or the other;
Around these parts
We oftentimes refer
To them as "Local Color".
They do some very silly things
As they go about their day
In fact, almost everything they do is
In some extraordinary way.
It's pretty entertaining
To see some of these things;
They might even attempt to fly,
And know they have no wings.
Some call their actions crazy,
A better word's unique;
But, in any case, I guarantee
The laughter will make you weak.

The Magnolia Tree

There's a majestic, old magnolia tree,
That stands in my front yard;
It's a tree that's grown there for ages,
And whose beauty you can't disregard.
She spreads her branches quite nobly,
And her stance is that of a queen;
She stretches her arms so commandingly,
As if certainly crying out to be seen.
She's the center of much activity,
And I know a squirrel family lives there;
I'm sure she affords them much comfort,
For her branches don't ever go bare.
There's so much that's gone on around her,
I'm sure that so much could be told;
But she keeps all her secrets well guarded,
And simply remains a sight to behold.

The Cat

There's a cat that sits on our front porch,
Every morning I see her face;
She doesn't even live with us,
But she acts like she owns the place.
She stretches and she lounges,
She prances all about;
She seems to say with those green eyes,
She thinks she could put us out.
Where did all this come from?
I think that's how all cats are;
They think we're all beneath them,
And they're the superior ones by far.

Soul Food Restaurant

When you frequent your favorite soul food spot,
Along with your faithful friends;
What you'll eat any given day,
On your tastes it all depends.
The selections are quite varied,
And the menu may read like this:
For breakfast: Country Ham and Eggs,
With Biscuits and Cheese Grits,
For Lunch: Neckbones, Catfish,
Smothered Chicken,
Pork chops and Pigs feet.
Everything looks so delicious,
And these are just the meats.
The vegetables you might enjoy,
Include greens, squash, and black-eyed peas;
Or you might want fried corn and pinto beans,
Along with macaroni and cheese.
Whatever it is that you decide,
It's sure to hit the spot,
It'll come delivered to your booth,
Fresh and piping hot.
Be prepared to sit a spell,
'Cause you won't want to move;
For you will have dined most sumptuously,
As your clean plate will prove.

Yardsaling

Yardsaling is a southern art,
And to some it's a way of life;
It's a way of getting almost anything,
Without the stress and strife.
You meet all kinds of people,
And you see how others live;
And while the kids sell lemonade,
You negotiate what you'll give.
There's always a faithful crew,
That gets up before the dawn;
To see what treasures they might find,
On some neighbor's lawn.
There's much anticipation
Of the next bargain 'round the bend;
And everyone knows in yardsaling ,
The possibilities never end.
There's always something
You've been searching for
Suddenly, staring you in the face;
And when your eyes lock on to it,
Your heart begins to race.
There's nothing like the yard sale game,
Or should I say, the sport ;
It quite easily becomes an addition,
If you're of that sort.

Country Living

Country Living

It's grassroots.
It's simple.
It's basic, not plush.
Uncomplicated .
Uncluttered.
Unhurried.
Unrushed.
It's relaxed.
Unpolluted.
Unequaled.
Unmatched.

A Country View

What might you see as you go your way
On a walk through the country any spring day?
There's an old car tire without its rim,
Filled with flowers to the brim.
A bottle tree glistens in the sun,
And kids chunk rocks at it just for fun.
A rusty pump stands waiting still,
For thirsty ones to get their fill.
Someone's hound dog saunters by,
And gives no notice
Till you catch his eye.
A rooster struts across the yard,
Catching him would be awfully hard.
A pickup truck putters down a dirt road,
The back is filled with a sumptuous load.
A tractor sits quietly in a farmer's field,
For sometime later to harvest a yield.
There are cows in the pasture,
That graze and chew;
While horses trot proudly for all to view.
A turtle creeps across the road,
And in the grass there hides a small toad.
Wild flowers sprout along every path,
Their sheer numbers defy any math.
Muscadines ripen on winding vines
And could possibly become
Someone's tasty sweet wine.
There's never a lack of quaint things to see,
And just imagine all this for free.

Country Breakfast

A real country po' folk's breakfast
Is in these days quite rare,
It's certainly not your typical
Bacon and egg type affair.
There'd be crispy fried chicken,
With all the parts there to eat;
The usual ones represented,
Plus the neck, back and feet.
There might be some country ham,
But not the thin sterile kind;
It's the thick, salty slices
From the smokehouse you'll find.
If you're lucky, there's rabbit,
From a recent hunt trip;
With juicy, brown gravy
That drips from your lips.
There would probably be rice,
With sugar and butter of course;
And big, chunky biscuits
That could choke any horse.
What goes in the middle,
Is anyone's guess;
Some molasses or syrup
Would sure pass the test.
But, most want preserves
From the cook's vast store;
From the past summer's canning,
In flavors galore.

The milk would be powdered,
And straight from a box;
There's likey no juice,
'til opportunity knocks.
But, we all know one thing
That's sure to be had;
It's a jug full of Kool-Aid,
And the flavor is
Red.

Let's

Let's go for a ride in the countryside,
And make lots of stops along the way;
Let's soak in all the warm sunshine,
And create a perfect day.
Let's stop at someone's roadside stand,
And maybe buy some fruit;
Let's pretend it's some great find,
Just like a pirate's loot.
Let's go inside a country store,
And have some bologna cut;
Let's sit outside and eat our fare,
Like some treasure from King Tut.
Let's always enjoy life's simple things,
And to their full extent;
Let's always spend these kinds of times,
And make it our intent.

Country Cure (All)

If the baby has the sniffles,
Or an all-out whooping cough;
If your throat is sore or neck's in pain,
And you need to throw it off;
If your chest is tight or breathing's bad
From some sort of pollution;
The answer's simple for country folk,
There is but one solution.
Vick's Salve is what they call it,
It's thought to cure most anything;
It's used for any malady,
From arthritis to bee sting.
It's the all purpose remedy,
And one you must endure;
If you voice any type of complaint,
It's Vick's for you for sure.
On chest or back
Or up the nose,
Even a teaspoon or two;
Country folks believe, without a doubt,
It'll cure what's ailing you.

Shelling Peas

It's summer time in the country,
And the kids buzz around like bees;
But, when that silver tub is placed on the porch,
It's time for shelling peas.
From the smallest to the oldest,
It's something we'd all do;
At first, of course, the little ones
Didn't have a clue.
They'd watch to see just how it went,
And soon ,they'd give a try;
Then look amazed at fingers stained,
As though dipped in purple dye.
When we'd first get started,
It seemed an insurmountable chore;
There looked like half a million peas,
Or maybe even more.
But, after we all got the flow,
We'd turn it into fun;
We'd have a race to see just who
Would be the first one done.
We'd each one have our own bowl,
And a paper sack;
We'd slip our fingers through the hull,
Then throw it empty back.
At last, when all the shells lay empty,
And a tub of peas was done;
We'd let the grown-ups take the haul,
Then look for some new fun.

Slopping Hogs

The farmer has a brood of hogs,
That he tends with special care;
He might even let you "slop" them,
If it's something that you'd dare.
There's usually one that's black and white,
One tan and one that's brown;
But, they usually all look just alike,
Lying muddied on the ground.
The farmer and his trusty dog
Will make their way with you,
To the hog pen where the brood awaits,
To slobber and to chew.
The food you'll serve is quite a mush
Of table scraps, corn and bread;
That's mixed together throughout the day,
To keep this crew well fed.
You must first get their attention,
Crying "Here Piggy" and "Suee Wee";
Then you pour your concoction in the trough
And fill it totally.
Soon, they all come rushing,
Snorting and rooting about;
They push and shove most mercilessly,
And a little one gets left out.
In no time at all, you're finished,
You've done this dirty deed;
And, hopefully, you didn't get splashed (too much),
As they feasted in their greed.

Hog Killing Time

There's a chill in the air
And holidays are near,
Thanksgiving's just 'round the bend;
There's a feeling amongst country folks
That's absolute prime,
Everyone senses it's hog killing time.
Oh, what a spectacle!
Oh, what a show!
You'll find nothing like it,
If you look high and low.
From sunup to sundown,
It lasts the whole day;
And once it gets started,
Horses couldn't pull you away.
Everyone has his own part to do,
With all the commotion,
It feels like a zoo.
The poor victim for this occasion
Has long been picked out,
And soon will become food,
From his tail to his snout.
There's a shot and a squeal
And he's out for the count;
A cut of the throat,
And blood spews like a fount.
In a barrel of hot water,
He's cleaned and de-haired,
Amongst all the men,
This giant task is shared.

A skillful knife separates all parts of meat,
Including pig ears, pig tail and pig feet.
The women's task is always chittlin's to
make .
There's a boatload of goo and muck
They must rake.
When nighttime falls,
All surround the black pot;
Where the oil is bubbling
And boy is it hot!
Pieces of skin are stirred with a surge,
And after some time,
Crisp cracklings emerge.
Sweet potatoes are roasted, right in the fire,
And of these simple treats,
No one ever does tire.
When it's all finally over,
And the day is all done;
The grown-ups are weary,
But the kids just had fun.

Making Cracklings

First, you have to kill a hog,
Then, carefully take off the skin;
Cut it up in little squares,
And then the fun begins.
Take a big, black, iron pot,
Then, put in some lard;
As you'll see, it's quite simple,
Nothing very hard.
You wait until the oil is bubbling
And it's boiling hot;
Then get the pieces that you've cut
And toss them in the pot.
Now, just stand around and tell some tales
And maybe a few jokes;
It's best when you've got a crowd,
Of good ole' country folks.
After some stirring and simmering,
The skins are crisp and puffed;
Then, you have a delicious treat,
Of which, you'll never get enough.

Preaching Sunday

In the old country church,
Preaching Sunday was quite a big deal;
In just a few words, I'll give you a feel.
White gloved ushers monitor each bench and pew,
Wearing uniforms starched to look like brand new.
Little girls decked out in ruffles and bows,
Sit with mothers in hats sharp
From their heads to their toes.
The minister quotes scriptures
With deep breaths
And a long pause,
He makes so dramatic each and every clause.
At the end of the message, when some hymn is sung,
Shouts ring out between every rung.
There's jerking and fanning and some falling out,
Small ones wonder what all the commotion's
about.
When everything's over and the service is done,
Everyone enjoys a grand feast on the lawn.

Baptismal Sunday

Sometimes in the country church,
when they had no baptismal pool,
Baptizing in a neighbor's pond,
was oftentimes the rule.
They'd gather all the candidates,
from all the months gone by,
Those who'd made a sacred vow,
to their old lives they would die.
The ones who were to be submerged
wore white robes and white caps,
They marched up to the waters edge,
some quite afraid, perhaps.
Prayers were said and hymns were sung,
and the preacher waded deep,
He'd call them in, one by one,
to take that faithful leap.
He'd raise his hand and say the words
"Father, Son and Holy Ghost",
Then dipped them in and raised them up,
witnessed by the crowded host.
There'd be someone who'd send up praise,
and someone who would shout,
And, almost predictably,
someone would fall out.
They'd fan the ones who'd "felt the touch"
and greet the new converts,
Then, make their way back up the road ,
to the country church.

Childhood Memories

Country Doctor

My dad was a country doctor
And I have such memories galore;
I even remember the house calls,
As he literally traveled 'round door to door.
Sometimes, on Saturday mornings,
When I was just a young thing;
My daddy would let me go with him,
As he did all his doctoring.
He'd have his black bag in one hand,
And his stethoscope wrapped 'round his neck;
He was most definitely the captain,
And I was his first man on deck.
We traveled way deep in the country,
And there were always such sites to see;
Believe you me, I noticed them all,
Down to the last bumblebee.
I'd always meet really kind people,
As I stayed close by my daddy's side;
He'd always give my introduction,
As he stood there beaming with pride.
Many of the people had no indoor plumbing,
And most of them were all very poor;
So my daddy would let patients pay him,
With whatever it was they'd procure.
Sometimes, he took brown eggs or slab bacon,
Fresh vegetables, hams and the like;
All of this was so amazing to see,
For me as such a young tike.

The old women, he'd always call "young lady",
But old and young all addressed him as sir.
We'd make so many stops on our journey,
I'm quite surprised that it's not all a blur.
I remember learning about all of these people,
And all of the crops that they grew.
Each time, I'd learn something different,
Each time, I'd learn something quite new.
My eyes would grow wide with excitement,
As I saw all the animals and stock;
We'd see so much beautiful scenery,
As we'd drive to our next door to knock.
My dad had such a busy schedule,
I can't imagine how he got it all done;
All I remember is I loved tagging along,
And all I remember is fun.

The Agnews

There was a family who lived right beside us,
Nine kids with their Mom and Dad;
I don't know what brought us together so close,
But, I tell you, I certainly am glad.
Almost everything I learned as a child,
Was learned with this lively crew;
Every new thing that I came to experience,
Was done with some Agnew.
Mary, the oldest, was the inspiration,
Of how far we all could go;
I mostly saw her going off to college,
With all her things in tow.
If you wanted to learn about kindness,
To Sula you would go;
She was the sweetest person in all the world,
That you could ever know.
Geneva was the Barbie Doll,
The ultimate girly girl;
She'd take great care with hair and nails,
And perfected every curl.
Larry was the big brother,
Strong, determined and quiet;
I remember him once losing lots of weight
When he went on a diet.
Rickey was the daredevil one,
And he taught me how to drive;
Down country roads, he'd let me try,
And we still came out alive.

Darlene showed me what all was possible,
For a girl to do;
She was smart, athletic and feminine
And she taught me to tie my shoe.
Ronnie taught me good study habits,
And he was probably my first crush;
Thinking back on the feelings I had,
Almost makes me want to blush.
Sharron and Darron were the youngest,
They were the fraternal twins;
We'd play and play and play all day,
And were the bestest friends.
Mrs. Agnew was an angel,
It's about all that I can say;
She helped to shape and mold my life,
In every imaginable way.
Mr. Agnew kept us all in line,
He was the greatest dad;
And when they moved (just up the road),
I was so very sad.

Mr. Agnew

Let me tell you about a man,
Who was like my second dad;
I was really almost as close to him,
As to the biological one I had.
Mr. Agnew was his name,
And he had a very large crew;
But, he always let me be included,
In everything they'd do.
The real experience of country life,
Is what I got from him;
Each and every memory's quite vivid,
Not a one of them has dimmed.
In the summer he'd take us all
To the truck patch to pick a load;
We'd make our way to the place,
Down a narrow, winding road.
Vegetables, vegetables everywhere,
Surrounded his kids and me;
There were peas and greens and other kinds
As far as the eye could see.
In the fall, he'd host the hog killings,
Many would come just to see;
And who was amongst all that crowd?
You guessed it, little ole' me.
In winter time it was to the smokehouse
He would go to get the meat;
At other times, his hunting trips
Would provide all kinds of treats.
He'd take us to the small bread store,
To get the day old bread;

He'd gather up quite a load,
To keep his family fed.
He'd carefully tend his garden,
As we stood by and looked;
He taught us lessons every day,
You couldn't find in any book.
He had a coup full of chickens,
And sometimes, we'd gather the eggs;
Quite often, one of those chickens
Would wind up on our plates,
As tasty fried chicken legs.
On Sundays he would take us all to church,
And there, he'd like to sing;
I even joined in with the family's group,
On Easter program in the spring.
He also thought himself a cook,
Fried okra was his specialty;
Coming out of the grease all peppered and hot,
It was the best, if you'd ever ask me.
His wife and he were quite a pair,
And before they went to bed;
We'd sit and watch as she lovingly
Scratched the dandruff from his head.

Childhood Christmas

Christmastime at our house
Was such a joyous thing;
There was much anticipation,
Of what the day would bring.
For many months prior,
The list making would begin;
There were so many things I wanted,
On pure memory I couldn't depend.
I carried handy 'round with me
A trusty little list,
There was not one single thing,
I wanted my parents to miss.
And every year, without a doubt,
I couldn't ask for any better,
For, I'd get everything on my list,
Down to the very letter.
The night before, my brother and I
Would always try our best;
To catch ole' Santa in his tracks,
So, we'd get little rest.
We'd try to keep ourselves alert,
With a flashlight by our side;
But, every year ole' St. Nick
Would cleverly by us slide.
We must have fallen fast asleep,
Before the morning's light;
Because our toys appeared, miraculously,
Sometime through the night.

In our den, the floor was covered,
With toys of every kind;
The sheer volume of them all,
Would surely blow your mind.
We'd jump around from here to there,
And squeal with pure delight;
We couldn't have concealed our excitement,
If we'd tried with all our might.
Later on in the day,
The relatives would pour in;
For the traditional Christmas dinner,
With us and all our kin.
We'd have such an array of food,
Usually, specialties of the South;
One year, we even had a whole roasted pig,
With an apple in his mouth.
We'd exchange gifts and laughter,
And each other's company enjoy;
The men would often help assemble
Some child's complicated toy.
Our festivities usually lasted
Way into the night;
And after all was said and done,
We felt everything went just right.

Alpha Parties

As a little girl, I remember
My dad and his fraternity friends
Would have some quite rambunctious parties
That seemed to never end.
There was always lots and lots of food,
And, of course, there was much strong drink;
More people filled our house those nights,
Than you could ever think.
Every room overflowed with folks,
Men and wives and, I guess, girlfriends;
The activities from room to room
Would, usually, just depend.
There was smoking and drinking,
And some card playing, too;
There was music and laughter
And some dancing to view.
Of course, as the hostess,
My mom mingled and floated about;
She was the ultimate hostess,
Of this, there's certainly no doubt.
I'm sure, better house parties
Had never been thrown,
And I'm sure they were the best
That those guests had all known.

Nature Lovers

My dad would teach me of nature,
He'd point out all of the trees;
And as we walked around in the yard,
He'd help me recognize all the leaves.
Looking out of our window,
He'd name all the birds there for me;
If an especially pretty one happened by,
He'd make sure that I'd see.
To this day, I'm thankful,
For all the insights he gave to me;
I think of them with every beautiful sunset
That I see.
I try to pass all this along,
To my only son;
I want him to notice all of God's works,
And appreciate every one.

C. C. Augustus Pool

Nearing May, we could hardly wait,
For the end of school;
Cause that surely meant for my friends and I,
We'd be headed to the pool.
It was, by far, our favorite way,
To pass away the time;
It didn't matter much at all,
If we had to scrape up every dime.
Of course, there was the swimming part,
But, it was more a social thing;
It was the place that we'd all meet,
And maybe start a summer fling.
There was always the finest lifeguards,
That you had ever seen.
They were the most buffed and well-built guys,
All muscled, toned and lean.
Over the years, just to name a few,
There was Malcolm, Ike and Kenny;
If I were to try to name them all,
The list would be too many.
We'd jump into the showers,
Then head out to the deck;
They'd all tell us not to run,
So we wouldn't break our necks.
There were snow cones and candy bars
And other treats to buy;
Everything was fairly priced,
And nothing was too high.

Sometimes, we'd run across the street
To Mr. Quick, to buy a thing or two;
About how we would come to miss those days,
We didn't have a clue.
We really did love that place,
From the time we were very young;
There'd be swimming lessons
During summer camp,
And pool parties where we hung.
There were activities both day and night,
And boy; we had such fun;
So, every year, we could hardly wait,
For that summer sun.

Poetry

My daddy helped me to love poetry,
He liked that kind of thing;
On Sunday mornings we'd recite,
"When Malindy Sings."
I loved the rhythm and the rhyme,
Each stanza and each verse;
We'd just say it how we felt,
With no need to rehearse.
I like to write my own poems now,
And let my own words flow;
I find that there are things inside,
I want other folks to know.
It's such a wonderful feeling,
To see my own words in print;
Sometimes, I think the words I write,
Are truly heaven sent.
Wherever it all comes from,
It's something I love to do;
It's my hope , in some small way,
It's most enjoyable to you.

My Dream

I had a most delightful dream,
One night, when I was young;
It's been so very long ago,
But in my memory, it has hung.
The old cow pasture, beside our house,
Was no longer just that;
It had become a candy land
And not an animal habitat.
There were candy canes everywhere
And huge lollipops galore,
Everywhere I looked around
There were more and more and more.
Everything was so beautiful,
It was such a magnificent sight;
Everything looked so cheerful,
And the colors were so bright.
There was a sparkling spring
And butterflies,
And even a unicorn;
I remember, it's snow white hair,
And it's delicate spiraled horn.
When I woke up, I hoped to see,
Again this lovely scene;
But, of course, it was not to be,
For, it was just a dream.

Double Life

I grew up as a country girl,
But, I had my city friends;
The activities of my daily life,
On which side it would depend.
With the country crew, I was a no shoe girl,
With hair wild upon my head;
I'd run and play and make mud pies,
Until I went to bed.
There were chickens and cows, goats and pigs,
Animals all around;
And somehow, everything we did,
Was connected with the ground.
We'd root around in the garden,
And go fishing in the pond;
We'd pick wild berries on the path,
And have all kinds of fun.
We'd walk along the dusty roads,
And eat the red clay dirt;
In the country, we always knew,
A little dirt could never hurt.
But, then, on the city side,
We'd mostly do house things;
We'd play with Barbies and paper dolls,
Or try on sparkly rings.
We'd play games or watch t.v.
Or walk along the street;
We might go to the corner store,
And other friends there greet.
I truly had a double life,
That's plain for all to see;
It was a unique way of life,
But one so right for me.

Neighborhood Groceries

Asby's
Mayhorn's
Cherry Street
Pickled Souse
Rag Bologna
Liver Cheese
Dill Pickles in a jar
Penny Cookies
Coconut
Chocolate Chip
And Butter
Stage Planks
Moon Pies
Apple Sticks
Tootsie Rolls
Point out what you want
Behind the glass.
Service with a smile.
Home folks you know.

Partyline

Do you remember
Picking up the phone...
"Excuse me"
"Could I make a call, please?"
"It's an emergency."
"Five minutes?"
"O.K."
"Thank You." Click.
Or listening in on some juicy gossip,
Or some steamy love talk late at night.
Easing up the receiver ...Slowly...Carefully...
(muffled giggles)
"Shhhhh"
"Be quiet, they'll hear us."
"Hey you kids, quit playing on the phone!"
"Uhhh..ohhhh, we're caught." Click.
Partyline.

Partlow's Band

Though, technically, it was Carver High School Band,
To one man it belonged;
 If you thought that there was any other rule,
Then, you'd be sorely wrong.
On game days, we all knew,
The band would give a show;
From the school, they'd make their start,
And down Green Street, they would go.
First, we'd hear those mighty drums,
And then, the marching feet;
The anticipation was so great,
As crowds lined along the street.
The majorettes were a sight to see,
In glittering blue and gold;
And little Gwen, who led the way,
Was maybe nine years old.
With batons twirling in the air,
And tassels wagging on their feet;
There was always a special show,
For each corner crowd they'd meet.
Each girl was stacked and built,
Not a one of them was boney;
They'd twist and turn and prance about,
And Gwen would do "the Pony."
Mr. Partlow, with head held high,
Would walk along the side;
He'd strut like some male peacock,
With confidence and pride.
Mr. Partlow has passed away, but, history does repeat;
His son's Partlow's Drummers carry on the torch,
With each resounding beat.

Reed's Dept. Store
(Established 1905)

Reed's Dept. Store in Tupelo,
Is the oldest in the town;
It was the place, as a child,
Where all my clothing needs were found.
Each year, in the fall, with my mom,
Before the start of school;
We'd go to Reed's for school attire,
This was just the rule.
When it was time for a winter coat,
It was off to Reed's we'd go;
So I'd be prepared for chilly days,
Or, maybe even snow.
Reed's is where we'd always get,
Our uniforms for scouts;
If we needed a new cap or sash,
Reed's would have it, without a doubt.
Over the years, it stayed the same,
If we had special needs;
For fancy occasions or big events,
We'd always go to Reed's.

Little Miss Perfect

I knew a little girl when I was young,
Who wore two pigtails across her head;
I thought she was the cutest thing,
And this, I often said.
Over the years, I watched her,
She was always quiet, likeable and smart;
To me, she seemed so perfect,
And had life down to an art.
She was always polite and mannerable,
And very popular in school;
She was the kind that teachers loved,
For she followed all the rules.
Now that we're much older,
She's still one that I admire;
She's a diligent wife, mother and church worker,
And seems to never tire.
I often say to her and friends,
That she's such a role model to me;
She always laughs and waves me off,
But, I'm as serious as I can be.
Back then, she was known as Damita Adams,
But, since marriage, her name's not the same;
Now, when I speak of Little Miss Perfect,
'Chelle Tucker is the name.

Family History

Thanks Mom and Dad!

I love you Mama and Daddy,
You've taught me oh so much;
I can't begin to describe all the ways
That my life you've profoundly touched.
You've taught me morals and values
You've helped me reach my goals
And all the things I've learned from you
Will stay till I am old.
I want to thank you deeply,
For being there for me;
And being absolutely, without a doubt,
The best parents ones could be!

Right to Vote

I love to hear the stories,
That my mama and daddy tell;
Sometimes, we'll just sit a while,
And they'll talk for a spell.
They've told me of how hard it was,
For them to get to vote;
They'd go down to the courthouse door,
And there would be a note;
"Out To Lunch" or "No One's In,"
"Come Back Another Day,"
In all kinds of ways you wouldn't believe,
They were turned away.
Even when they did get in,
There were more hurdles they had to cross;
They'd be asked to answer questions
That would put anyone at a loss,
"How many bubbles in a bar of soap?"
"How many pennies in that jar?"
"How many raindrops to fill a barrel?"
"How many miles to a star?"
It seems almost incredulous
That this was how it was;
But, believe you me, no matter what,
I vote, now, just because.

One Room School

My mother told me stories,
Of the one room school;
Where all the grades were taught together,
As they went by the same rules.
To this school is where she would go,
With other children from all around;
Traveling there in rain, sleet or snow,
These children could be found.
Each grade had their own lessons,
That they were all to learn;
While keeping warm by an old black stove,
That in the corner burned.
My mother has high praises
For the teacher who taught them there,
Because, it was her own dear mother,
Who gave them special care.
My mother said that in this place,
She learned so very much;
Like arithmetic and writing,
Basic reading skills and such.
I love to hear these stories,
Over and over again,
For in passing them on down the line,
Our legacy never ends.

Alton Odessa Kilgore

I never knew my grandfather Alton,
But I'm told he was a very smart man.
Everyone called him professor;
And of learning, he was quite a big fan.
His parents sent him off to college,
And he was the principal of a one room school,
He taught the children lovingly,
And he laid down all the rules.
He was my mother's father,
And the father of seven more;
He produced a family of very bright kids,
All with the name Kilgore.

Henry

My son's name is Henry,
It's the only name he could be;
He looks and talks and acts
Just like a Henry to me.
His grandfather's name is Henry (James Henry),
And his uncle's a Henry too (Brian Henry).
Three of his great-grandfathers
Were even Henrys, too.
He had a great uncle Henry,
He's one we can't forget;
And I'm sure on down the line,
There are other Henrys, yet.
I hope that Henry will wear with pride,
This name that is his lot,
And always hold most dear to him,
The strong heritage that he's got.

Know It All (He thinks)

My son, Henry Dorsey,
Knows about everything there is. (He thinks)
If a question needs an answer,
The right one is always his. (He thinks)
Please don't try to argue,
Because he is always right; (He thinks)
You could never sway him from his view,
If you tried with all your might.
No matter what the subject,
He can tell you right away; (He thinks)
All you need to know about anything
On any given day.
Henry's got to be the smartest boy,
The world has ever seen;
Because he has the answer to everything,
(He thinks)
And he's not yet in his teens.

Getting Personal

Name Calling

Patty, Patty Cake, Patsy,
Tisha, Trisha, Trish;
I've got more names that I am called,
I can't even begin to list.
My family and most Mississippi friends say Pat,
My husband says Patricia;
I answer to both names the same,
It doesn't raise an issue.
Patricia's such a simple name,
And lots of females have it;
But, you couldn't imagine all the names,
That people make up from it.

Inside Me

Inside me,
A well springs eternal,
Hopes and dreams take flight,
Poems spew forth like a fountain,
Flowers bloom in bright colors,
Butterflies spread their wings,
And new life awaits.
Inside me,
There's a barefoot girl in pigtails,
A woman in silk stockings and high heels,
A sophisticated lady of the day,
And a sultry lady of the evening,
There's a church goer and a party thrower,
There's somebody's mother, daughter, sister,
Wife, lover and friend;
There's all of that
Inside me.
Can you see it?

Loving Me

I've always loved how I'm made,
It's always seemed so right to me;
Ever part is just in place,
How it ought to be.
I've always loved my honey skin,
And my thick, coarse head of hair.
If I could change it all today,
I'm sure I wouldn't dare.
Since I was in my early teens,
I've been five feet six;
It's not too tall and not too short,
So, there's nothing there to fix.
I'm so proud of nature's gifts,
Everything's as it should be;
And put together as it is,
Is just what makes me ....me.

Happy (With The Nappy)

I'm happy with the nappy.
My hair's real thick.
Roots get tough.
Edges get rough.
My man calls it coarse,
And he says he likes it.
Sometimes, the comb gets stuck.
But, when my man runs his fingers
Through my hair,
It feels like silk.
So............
I'm happy with the nappy.

Boston
(Language Barrier)

In my eighteenth year, I went off to Boston,
To finish up with school;
I packed my things and headed north,
To enter the college pool.
There was one thing I soon found out,
The language was not the same;
If I wanted some very simple thing,
They'd have some strange, new name.
When I wanted a milkshake, plain and clear,
"Frappe" was the name they had;
"What's going on," I'd think out loud,
"Has all the world gone mad?"
They'd say the word was "tonic,"
When I wanted a soda pop;
I really couldn't believe my ears
This madness had to stop.
Whenever I would order food,
It seemed that just to eat,
I needed some kind of interpreter;
For it was such a feat.
But, regardless of the name they'd give,
I'd say it the southern way;
And I'll bet those folks remember it still,
To this very day.

Too Cold For Comfort

When I went off to school in Boston,
I realized why Southerners have a slower pace;
When the weather's not so frigid out,
There is no need to race.
When the weather's nice and toasty,
You can take time to slowly walk;
When you don't feel you'll freeze to death,
With your friends, you can casually talk.
Northerners don't really know what it is ,
To take a leisurely stroll;
They're always rushing here or there,
'Cause the weather's just too cold.

The Hook up

A very close friend of mine,
Called me up one day;
And said, "I have the man for you,
You must meet him right away."
She said, "He attends church regularly,
And his contribution is good, too.
I just know I've found the man,
The perfect one for you."
"Blanche," I said, " I think, I'll pass,
I don't believe in blind dates;
There has to be something amiss,
I think that I'll just wait."
"Does he have a car and a job?"
"Does he live with his mother?"
"If he filled out an application
For sex, would he check OTHER?"
She said, "Come on, just trust me,
I wouldn't steer you wrong;
I know you'll fall in love with him,
And I'll be singing your wedding song."
"O.K., O.K., I'll meet him,
But don't expect anything at all;
One date is all I'll commit to,
And yes, you can tell him he can call."
A long story short, we had the date,
And it didn't go very well;
I was very much a tyrant,
But by his response, you'd never tell.

At the end of the evening,
He asked for a second date;
I couldn't believe the confidence,
"Wow, he'd make someone a good mate."
Well, now its been fourteen years,
And, guess what?
We're still together.
Sometimes, in life,
What we think we want
Doesn't really even matter.

Tupelo

The small town where I am from,
Gets its name from the Tupelo Gum.
No matter where in the world
That I might roam;
This is the place
That I call home.
Though I've been northeast for my education,
I've stayed fiercely Southern
In dedication.
In Memphis, I lived for many years,
By my own election,
And even still, there was that Tupelo connection.
At Elvis' Graceland,
Fans come to mourn;
But it's Tupelo, Mississippi,
Where he was born.
Tupelo is known as the All-American City
If you've never enjoyed it
That's quite a pity.
It's so warm, so hospitable and so neat,
Everything about it to me is so sweet.
I love the trees, the flowers and birds,
I can't really describe all its beauty in words.
Though many places in my life
Have played a significant part;
It's Tupelo, Mississippi, ya'll,
That still has all my heart.

My Sorority

You know us by the pink and green,
And the air of style and grace;
You'll probably notice a quiet confidence,
Plastered on each face.
Founded at Howard University,
It was the first one of it's kind;
The first African-American sorority,
The others came on down the line.
Alpha Kappa Alpha is the name,
It's a name I'm proud to share;
With some of the most distinctive women,
You'll find anywhere.

Shades of Lovely
(Good Enough to Eat)

Women of color are a sight to behold,
It's amazing to see their delicious colors unfold.
Honey,
Spice,
Brown Sugar,
Brown Rice,
Nutmeg,
Cinnamon,
Gingerbread and
Toast,
These are just a few of the colors,
That Black women boast.
There's Pecan, Almond, Walnut and Coconut Cream;
There are more shades than any could dream.
If chocolate's your weakness, they have every hue,
White chocolate, Dark chocolate and
Milk chocolate too.
They come in Caramel and they come in Toffee,
They even come like you like your coffee.
There's coffee with cream and coffee black,
Of any variety, there's certainly no lack.
There's Espresso
And Mocha
And Café au lait,
Too many colors to count in a day.

From Banana
To Licorice,
Including Hot Fudge;
If prizes were given,
Who could possibly judge?
When you see women of color,
In all their array;
There's nothing more lovely,
You'd just have to say.

Bookworm

Reading is fundamental,
That's what they always say;
Without it, I couldn't even imagine,
Wanting to start the day.
My mother's love of reading,
Was passed down straight to me;
And wherever it is that I am,
Some book with me, you will see.
In my purse, under my arm,
Or maybe in my car;
I'm not so sure where the book would be,
But it couldn't be very far.
My mother says she remembers,
Books and papers 'round her mother's bed;
Where she would spend the whole long day,
With knowledge being fed.
I love to read all kinds of things,
I never get enough;
I guess I could live without my books,
But , boy, it would be tough.

Salvation

As a child, I was so curious,
About religious things;
I'd buy so many Bible books,
And to each word I'd cling.
I wanted, quite desperately,
To know what path to take;
Somehow, I wanted explained to me,
How a right decision I could make.
I learned the keys were quite simple,
Once they were taught to me;
Hear, Believe, Repent, Confess,
Be Baptized;
It was quite clear to see.
So, into the church of Christ I was baptized,
Obeying without a doubt;
Then, finally, I knew at last,
What salvation was all about.

Brother Jones
(William Jones)

There is a preacher in the church,
Who, to me, preaches sermons just right;
He pulls in all the essential elements,
And there's never an oversight.
He explores the subject matter,
And, of course, it's full context;
And he makes it all so interesting,
That you wonder what comes next.
Using all very sound doctrine,
He strives to meet the needs;
He is a master at his job,
Of the flock to feed.
He makes you think, he makes you feel,
And he makes you ponder;
But, of the true meaning of any text,
He makes sure,
You never have to wonder.
He explains the background, Greek meanings,
And the history ;
He exegetes quite fully,
So there remains no mystery.
He incorporates poems and songs and quotes,
And he does it , oh so well;
To make it all applicable,
In this he never fails.
Again, I say, that he's a master,
Of his job, his craft, his art;
And it certainly could go without saying,
This man is very smart.

Act Two

There's something that's not much talked about,
But, it's quite a marvelous thing;
A woman in her midlife has a second spring.
Her feelings start to blossom,
Old things are made new;
She feels a certain vigor,
And a playfulness too.
It's a time when she comes alive again,
It's a joyous time for her;
The way she feels is so divine,
It makes her want to purr.
The reason I can tell you this,
My own experience is where it's from;
And there is one thing I know for sure,
The best is yet to come.

◆ ❖ ◆ ❖ ◆

Turning 40

When I turned 40,
I felt so brand new;
I bought a bikini,
And got a tatoo;
For some unknown reason,
I felt more alive;
I can't imagine what'll happen,
When I turn 45.

Warm and Fuzzy

Some Like It Hot......
But I like it warm.
I like Warm sunshine,
Warm tropical climates,
Warm blankets,
Warm hugs,
Warm handshakes,
Warm hospitality,
Warm greetings,
Warm gatherings,
Warm people,
Warm heartfelt emotions,
Warm rounds of applause,
And Warm Fuzzy Feelings.
Some Like It Hot.......
But, I like it warm.
Warm is real, real nice.

Intimacies

Waxing Poetic

My man told me that I have talent
And that I needed to share it with the world;
I just laughed and went on my way.
I don't do nothing but write down some words.
Don't nobody want to read that stuff.
He said,
You do.

◆ ❖ ◆ ❖ ◆◆

The (Un) Domestic Diva

I don't cook and I don't sew,
And I can hardly make a bed;
I don't even grocery shop,
To keep my family fed.
My friends are always wondering,
And often ask what it is I do;
Now, I can just simply say,
I write sweet poems for you.

Hearing Things

He says, "Hey girl,"
When he answers my call
And in that, I hear:
"I'm glad you called."
"I was missing you."
"I couldn't wait to hear your voice".
"You make me so happy."
"I love you so much."
Do you think he means all that ?
Doesn't matter.
That's what I hear.

♦ ❖ ◆ ❖ ♦♦

The Artist

Like Lady sang the blues,
Like Satchmo blew his horn,
Like Langston wrote his poems,
Like Satchel threw that ball,
Like Bojangles clicked his heels,
Like Thurgood tried a case,
Like Martin spouted words,
Like Ali circled the ring,
Like Mahalia delivered a hymn,
I love a man.
It's an art, Baby.

Simple Tastes

What does he like in a woman?
He likes a woman who's
Graceful...and tasteful
A woman who is nice...with some spice
A woman who is sunny...and funny
A woman who is insightful...and delightful
A woman who is kind...and has a sharp mind
A woman who is girly...and not burly
A woman who is smart...and a bit of a tart.
Most of all, he likes a woman...
Who is all woman,
And cannot be mistaken for anything else.
If you ask him what he likes in a woman,
He'll tell you to look at me.

Avid Reader

I want to be
Your favorite book,
That you read
Over and over again,
From cover to cover,
And get lost in the story.
Not a fairy tale.
Not a mystery.
No cliff hangers.
Just
A Plain
Old Fashioned
Love Story

Cry Baby

I cry at weddings,
I cry at funerals,
I cry when I watch them
Whip Kunta Kinte on Roots
To make him say 'his name.'
I always cry when something
Touches my heart,
And when my man
Touches my core.

Our Place

There is a place of enchanted love,
Where only you and I do dwell;
A place that's quiet and warm and safe,
A place that none can tell.
It's a very special, private place,
A place that no one knows.
It's a place of tender kisses,
Of knowing hearts and minds;
A place of wonderful delights,
And marvels of all kinds.
A place where we move in a timeless rhythm,
To the beat of our own drums;
A place where emotions flood our souls,
And to which we must succumb.
It carries us through time and space,
Where love can never end;
A sacred place that's so divine,
Where man and woman blend.
It's a place I want to dwell forever...
Just you and me alone;
A solemn place where love is shared,
Like none has ever known.

Summing Things Up

If Mississippi's In You

If Mississippi's in you,
It'll always be that way;
It matters not how far you go,
Or how long you stay.
If Mississippi's in you,
It always plays a part;
In how you live and move and breathe,
And in every notion of the heart.
If Mississippi's in you,
It's in you through and through;
It's who you are and how you be,
And it's in everything you do.
If Mississippi's in you,
There is some special glow;
A different something down inside,
That all the home folks know.
If Mississippi's in you,
It'll always be that way,
From the time you enter in the world,
Till in the grave you lay.
Every true Mississippian,
Can surely have it said:
"I'm Mississippi born,
I'm Mississippi bred,
And when I die ,
I'll be Mississippi dead."

Mississippi Through and Through

I could not be more a part of
the Mississippi landscape,
If I had sprouted right
out of the soil in some farmer's garden,
Or bloomed from a magnolia tree
in the yard of some plantation home,
Or emerged, like Venus, from the murky waters
of some catfish pond.
I breathe Mississippi.
I move Mississippi.
I think Mississippi.
I feel Mississippi.
I am, simply,
Mississippi through and through.

Reflections of a Mississippi Magnolia

When I look back on my life,
I think how wonderful it has been;
To have had the most wonderful parents of all,
And a host of wonderful friends.
My high school days were blissful,
And my college days so fun;
Fond memories are one thing for sure,
That I have by the ton.
I'm so glad I grew up,
On Mississippi sod,
My t-shirt reads: "American by birth,
And Southern by the grace of God."
My life has been so wonderful,
I wouldn't change one condition;
As one friend of mine always says,
I should have paid admission.

Mississippi Magnolia

Home is where the heart is,
That's what they always say;
Well, my heart is Mississippi's,
In the most profoundest way;
It's who I am,
It's what I like,
It's everything to me;
A Mississippi Magnolia girl
Is all I'll ever be.

◆ ❖ ◆ ❖ ◆

Diamonds are nice,
And so are pearls;
But, there's nothing on earth,
Like a Mississippi girl.

Unknown

◆ ❖ ◆ ❖ ◆